THE BOOK
OF STORIES

ROXANNA CARROTHERS

ISBN-13: 978-0-9968782-5-8

WE

ARE ALL

STORIES

IN THE

END

DEDICATED TO THE STORYTELLERS AND THEIR LISTENERS

.

PREFACE

This is a book of stories. People's stories and experiences that have led them to the belief that life is a journey of continuation....from cradle to grave and back to the place we came from.

There is no death, only a change of worlds.

Chief Seattle

There are no chapters in this book. Each section is an individual's story in their own words.

The exception being the story called Mary. Her story is one told through the ages and into today. Hers is a story of research and a personal experience of Her presence in the author's life today. Her influence is in several stories as She has impacted the lives of several people in the author's circle of friends. The explanation for this will be seen in Her story.

"All I have seen teaches me to trust the Creator for all I have not seen."

Ralph Waldo Emerson

I have used this quote in my first book and I use it again as nothing else can more accurately describe the stories in this book.

What all the contributors have been privileged to

i

experience are the doors of heaven opening long enough to give us a glimpse of the other side. A message of hope from the people we have lost here, expressing to us the truth that they continue and still are involved in our lives.

The doors to Heaven are indeed open in this age, demonstrated by the various messages that are being given to all people who are searching for something more than the existence in a one-dimensional world.

I know now that nothing has carried me up into the life of God or done more to open out the infinite meaning of love, than the fact that love can span this break of separation, can pass beyond the visible and hold on right across the chasm.

Rufus Jones

Harry Houdini comes to mind, who announced that if any way was possible for someone to come back, then he would most certainly do it. I wonder how often he appeared to those who loved him in everyday occurrences. Instead they were seeking a sign through mediums and discovered the money and time spent was a fool's mission. Harry had already spent most of his life proving that a great number of mediums were very challenged in their ability to contact the other side. From the following stories I hope to show that when the door to heaven is open and a sign of love is meant for you.....an intermediary is not needed.

I do believe that while I have met mediums who have a gift of seeing beyond and their ability to communicate with the other side, some of my most precious gifts have not needed interpretation, as they were direct and the sender left no doubt who was sending it.

Nothing is more powerful than being blessed to be in the presence of someone receiving a sign of love. In Karen Malcolm-Smiths story several people were there when she received an answer for her prayers

What I have found for myself, through these stories, is a general theme of love and compassion flowing, like a river, into the lives of people who have a deep connection with those on the other side.

He knows your name and He is allowing the love that exists with Him in a place we call Heaven, to send nuggets of love and messages that they are there, with Him. Also, apparent is the understanding that they are still very much involved in our lives that they still love us and it is apparent that we are and will be …. *family forever.*

Isn't that worth exploring the possibility?

The stories and pictures are all authentic and have not been enhanced or altered in any way, outside of editing the individual stories for grammar and spelling. The stories range from the sublime to the Divine.

All of these stories have the purpose of sharing with you a truth that life is a continuation. As you journey through the stories perhaps it will awaken a memory, a smell, a dream, a photograph or an experience that stirred your soul. Or perhaps you will now be open to the possibility that someone is reaching out to you if you care to participate in the experience they are offering you.

If so, the book will have served a purpose that will guide you through the rest of your journey with the knowledge that life continues on into infinity.

I have started the first story, in this journey of stories, with one personal to me. It involves many elements of so many other stories, with one exception. Steve, my son-in-law, lived with the knowledge that his time was limited to 12 to 13 months after his diagnosis of a brain tumor.

I chose it first as Steve was the epitome of patience and kindness to everyone in those few short months that he lived with the knowledge that his days were limited and precious. He had a bucket list and he was able to check off all of the important things before he left.

He never lost his faith. He never lost his love for God. He knew where he was going and he was at peace with it. He was the bravest of all of us on this journey with him. Because his journey also became my journey of supporting and loving him as his mother-in-law, while he taught me so much. I saw his true character under the most awful circumstances. I actually came to respect and love him more in those short months.

His story involves the gifts of grace that we all were exposed to in those months. They made me and so many of us secure in the knowledge that he was in the hands of love, kindness and gentleness. We also were given so many signs that he was only leaving us temporarily. As many that were on this side that wanted to keep him here with us, the messages were clear they were preparing a place on the other side, where he would be free of the disease that would take his life.

I have started *The Book of Stories* with Steve's story and I will end with Elizabeth Kubler-Ross. She was privy to many near death experiences of children. She wrote the book, *On Death and Dying*. Children who cross over and come back are incapable of dramatizing their stories. They tell their experience straight forward…..real, raw and awe-inspiring. If you doubt adults…listen to the children….they shall lead us.

STEPHEN SCHAD

THE BUS

In July of 2014, Steve was driving to work and felt extremely disoriented. There were no other signs of a problem up until that day. He called his wife, my daughter, and told her he needed her to come and get him. He had almost run another car off the road that he had failed to see, until he was on top of it.

My daughter picked him up and headed to the hospital. He was examined and quickly transferred from the hospital in their home town to a larger hospital in Milwaukee about 60 miles away.

After some tests with doctors in Milwaukee, the family and Steve were advised that Steve needed immediate surgery for a brain tumor. No one could absorb how fast our worlds were spinning. Strangers were now the most important people in our world. What had been important a day ago seemed so insignificant now.

The following is a message that woke Steve after his surgery before anyone saw the doctors. He felt compelled to share his vision and get it written down as soon as possible. True to his nature, he always thought of others first.

Introduction

This is a deep thought, dream or spiritual message that awoke me in July 2014 the night before I was diagnosed with terminal brain cancer. It is called "The Bus." I believe this was a spiritual message that I needed to hear to prepare for this part of my journey in this life, to try to keep a positive attitude. I also believe God wants me to share this message.

The Bus

"We are all on a journey through life and we have a choice where to sit on the bus and view it from."

God is steering the bus and only He knows the route we must take. Always remember it isn't just my journey but everyone's journey together.

The Different Views from Different Seats

1. The seats over the rear axle or hump

    a. These seats can be fun when you hit bumps and you bounce off the seats.
    b. These seats can get annoying after a while and even make you sore if you sit too long.

2. The side window seats

    a. You are only seeing ½ the journey and missing the other half.
    b. Staring too long out the side windows can be hypnotizing and make you feel alone and make your mind wander.

3. Looking out the rear window from the back seats.

    a. You can't prepare yourself for the things ahead.
    b. If you see something you like, you already went past it
    c. All you can hope for is it follows you and you get another chance.
    d. Staring out the back window can make you feel you are on this journey alone.
    e. You don't see the journey unfold before you if you only look out the rear window.

4. Looking out the windshield from the seats in the front of the bus

    a. You will see many things from the windshield seats that you won't see from other seats.
    b. You will see the sun rises and sunsets.
    c. You will see the beautiful views and have time to enjoy them before they pass.

d. You can sometimes see storms before you get there. You can't stop them, but at least you can try to prepare for them.

e. You can see when you are climbing a hill or when you are going to coast.

f. You will see accidents, tragedy and devastation

g. During these times you will also see people helping people, friendships being made, aid coming in to help.

h. Some amazing things can be seen and heard but you have to be patient.

i. Keep your eyes, ears, mind and heart open. These are the seats of positive thought on the bus you see who get on and off. Take the time, even if for only a moment, to introduce yourself, share a laugh, shed a tear, hold a hand or just listen.

"This is what we need to focus on to help us through difficult times. Stay looking forward. It is the only way to get through After all, this is our journey together."

Traveling together is a lot more fun than traveling alone.

"There is a reason for this."

---

5. There are no seatbelts on a bus and the seats are wide.

a. I believe we should share our seat, move around, see things from different views and let people know about the view from the windshield.

6. None of us really know when our journey ends but they all
    do.

    a. There may be time when you see the gauge close to
        "E" but only God knows how many mpg's the bus
        gets, where the next fuel stop is, how many hills to
        climb, how many times we coast, how many people
        get on and off the bus. An important thing to
        remember is, God will always let you on the bus. So
        enjoy the journey together.

"Love-Laugh-Share-Be Gentle and Kind"

Stephen R. Schad

After surgery the family was all taken into a room outside
of Steve's hearing. We were given the diagnosis that Steve would
have a few months to live. He was diagnosed with a glioblastoma
multiforme (GBM) tumor. They had removed what they could but
it was incurable. Steve knew the news couldn't be good, since
they took all of his family out the room. While a doctor was with
us, the surgeon was giving Steve the news. When we returned to
the room, we all had the devastating news. Steve was so worried
about us, it exemplified who he was. He wanted to comfort us.

Steve lived 13 months after his surgery. He lived those

months in the front of the Bus. He had a bucket list and did everything on it, in spite of debilitating treatments of medicine, radiation and chemotherapy. He exemplified love in his care and concern for others above his own needs. Perhaps his son said it best at Steve's funeral….."Cancer may have killed him, but it didn't take his life. He *lived* every moment up until his final breath."

Dragonflies

When walking outside in the yard during Steve's illness, I was struck by the number of dragonflies that filled the air. The property had been in the family for over 30 years and never had I witnessed the number of them in such close proximity to the house. As I have been made aware of the significance of signs all of my life, I looked up the meaning of dragonflies.

Dragonflies are a symbol of transformation and change.

In Native American legends, the dragonfly is a symbol of resurrection and renewal after hardship.

It is believed that big things are going to happen when you spot a dragonfly. They also are a symbol of impending death, spiritual souls who have passed and angels visiting. So I was particularly interested in the vast numbers that were hovering in between the pond and the house.

I interpreted this to mean that we were being given the sign of what was to come and that preparations were in the process somewhere beyond our view and understanding, but Steve was being tended to by the unseen.

—∞◦⟨⟨⟩⟩◦∞—

After Steve's passing the dragonflies were not seen in such massive numbers. I never really noticed them at all anymore. The house was a beehive of activity, with people coming and going for several days.

As I was leaving the house with Steve's son Bennett and my daughter, we saw that on a lawn chair, on the deck, was perched a magnificent red dragonfly! It was impossible not to notice as he was perched at eye level immediately after exiting the back door. He sat facing us and remained still while we all took pictures with our phones.

My next task was to look up the specific meaning of a red dragonfly. I found the following:

Red dragonflies can be rare to view. Yet, interestingly, they often appear to people surrounding life episodes of loss and death. Red dragonfly symbolism and death are intimately entwined as the end of life's illusion through transformation.

I would encounter the red dragonfly one more time in an intimate situation. A few years later I had the opportunity to visit my friend Sylvana, who was in her home and under the care of hospice. She had arranged alone time with each friend. This was my opportunity to visit and tell her goodbye. When I left her home after our intimate visit, I got to experience the joy of seeing a red dragonfly darting about a small waterfall structure outside her door. I knew preparations were already underway for her departure and *arrival*.

ST. JOSEPH

After Steve first entered the hospital and got his diagnosis of a terminal brain tumor and the shock of his diagnosis began to slowly sink in, I went to the gift shop to find something that may have some meaning to him.

Steve was a very spiritual person and in his youth had considered becoming a priest. He always had a deep sense of God and a deep love of God and that relationship was evident. He never ate a meal without giving thanks for what he was about to eat. Most amazingly he never ceased this practice even in the most devastating throes of his illness and treatments.

While at the gift shop, I was hoping to find a Mary or St. Francis statue but the only statue available was St. Joseph. Rather than leaving with nothing, I purchased it as a gift for Steve. My thought was St. Joseph was a father, a carpenter and devout husband. As Steve was a builder, painter, father and devout husband, I thought it would be appropriate.

I vaguely remembered a reading that I had with world renowned psychic George Anderson, after the loss of my son years before. George had explained that he had seen St. Joseph at the time of my son's death, which signified a peaceful passing. My daughter immediately remembered what St. Joseph had meant from my reading and was upset. She wanted to know if that had been why I had purchased it. I explained it was the only one in the gift shop and all the other things it meant to me.

Many weeks later my daughter, Steve and I were all at their church picnic. It was a wonderful event and we were all in high spirits that day! There was wonderful food, church friends and raffle items. At the end of the day some of the gift baskets that hadn't been won were being sold at a reduced price. I purchased three of the gift baskets. Two were wrapped in cellophane and the contents were visible. One had the theme of making salad with a recipe book, dressings, a lettuce washer and little items that added to a salad. The second basket was a movie, popcorn and movie candy. The last basket was wrapped completely and the contents weren't visible. I was excited, as I always loved the surprise of a white elephant. On our ride home I removed the wrapping and exposed an assortment of items that all related to St. Joseph. A small statue, a book about his life and another pamphlet about the many things he represents. I believe I received the gift of knowing how I was to direct my prayers.

RTL

The last story I shall share about Steve and his legacy is under the caption **RTL**. REFUSE TO LOSE.

Both of Steve's sons, Brandon and Bennett, had wrestled throughout their school years. Steve and Bobbi (our daughter) always attended their matches and were great supporters of the sport throughout all of the years they participated. They served food for the booster club, rode all over the country to matches and were their boy's biggest fans. Brandon continued wrestling into college and his parents were there whenever they were able.

Steve had devised a gimmick for the boys, an incentive that I believe was uniquely his idea. He wrapped the boys' two fingers with white adhesive tape and on the outside wrote in black marker; RTL (Refuse to lose). So when their hands were palms down on the wrestling mat, the letters were staring at them and reminding them to not give up or give in, but to continue to fight!

During Steve's illness Brandon had black wrist bands made up for family and friends with neon letters of RTL embossed on them. We're still wearing them and whenever I encounter someone with any type of struggle I tell them this story and give them a band to wear.

Bits and Pieces

Near death experience - (NDE) – is a personal experience associated with death or impending death. Such experiences may encompass a variety of sensations including detachment from the body, feelings of levitation, total serenity, security, warmth, the experience of absolute dissolution, and the presence of light.

I will not endeavor to report any negative NDE's, as by far the most popular and the majority of those experiences are positive.

Many movies and books have been written about the varied experiences of NDE. A favorite of mine is "Return from Tomorrow" by George Ritchie. Or perhaps my favorites are the many reported by family and friends that were experienced at the bed sides of their loved ones.

My father experienced many journeys away from the bed he was laying on prior to his passing, such as dancing with children, visiting with his long gone relatives and smiling in anticipation of his reunion with those places and people, that only he could see.

Kenneth Ring (an NDE researcher) has identified a consistent set of value and belief changes associated with people who have had a near-death experience. Among those changes, he found a greater appreciation for life, higher self-esteem, greater compassion for others, less concern for acquiring material wealth, a heightened sense of purpose and self-understanding, desire to learn, elevated spirituality, greater concern for all mankind and the planet, and a feeling of being more intuitive.

Roxanna Carrothers

JOE T

Joe wished to remain anonymous for personal reasons, but we thank him for bravely sharing his story.

There is a good reason I don't like to tell this story. There aren't any words in the human language to describe what I experienced when I went to heaven...or what I felt. All I can really say is that it was real.

And the feeling that will stay with me forever is so deeply grounded in the certainty of eternal life that I am no longer afraid to die or to lose any of my children. This life is not the end.

On the day after Christmas in 2012, I was medevac'd from a small rural community, 120 miles away to the city of Anchorage, Alaska. Getting there was a blur, but I found myself in the ICU unit in the worst pain of my life. I had a massive heart attack at age 59. A *"Widow's Maker"* heart attack, they told me, from a major blockage. It is almost always fatal without emergency care. With a wonderful wife and five children under the age of 11 at home, I was terrified.

Even at that moment, I can't say that I turned to God for help. I was a believer, but I was trying to find the connection between science and God's hand in the world. The problem of correlating the two thoughts often consumed me with no resolution. As an ER and ICU nurse for 40 years, I had witnessed the reality of death and dying, which left me a practical thinker.

Sometime during the surgery, I was suddenly standing at the window of the hospital room. My body was on the bed but the conscious me was staring out of the window observing the unseasonably warm winter temperatures melt the snow and ice, as water dripped from the roof. I felt free of the excruciating pain and at peace. There were figures walking around the room, maybe doctors and nurses, I couldn't make out their faces or their shapes. They seemed to be an insignificant part of was happening to me and soon they all began to fade away.

The next thing I knew, I was in a garden. Whatever the words I try to use in an attempt to describe what I saw, pales in comparison to what it really was. There were fields of what appeared to be trees and flowers separated by a path. They were so vibrantly brilliant and illuminating but not a color I could identify as having ever seen before.

An amazing luminous light filled the garden….so brightly radiant yet it didn't affect my vision. At the same time I was warm and comfortable. I can't recall if the light was radiating towards me or if I was traveling into it. My body was weightless and free. The euphoria was beyond words.

I thought I knew where I was going without being able to identify it. It was a place that I had been before though and it felt as if I was coming back. It was as though I had finally made it.

I was stopped at a place along the path and greeted by my grandmother and my aunt. I had never met my aunt. She died as a child before I was even born. But I knew her and she knew me. She was clapping and jumping and so full of joy that I was there! There were many figures in the distance, figures that didn't have clarity but we all knew each other. They seemed to be connected to the light but with distinction in their arms and limbs; an unexplainable perfection. I knew I belonged here with every fiber of my being.

---

*Being met with such love is an
indescribable feeling.*

Softly, my *gramma* pulled back a translucent veil that was a shade darker than the radiant light; a barely visible curtain that was oddly separating us. The moment I took a step to cross through the veil, the thought came to me that I would not go back to my children.

Was God giving me a choice or was He sending me back? Because in a flash, I was suddenly laying on the hospital bed in agonizing pain.

Five years later, I think about how that little glimpse into a world beyond has changed my way of thinking. I don't feel the need to measure the common denominator of science against the wonders of God's work anymore. When I go to church, everything takes on a different and deeper meaning. I know that the "truth" is real and I know what comes after this life. Sometimes I get angry that I am still here, when I know what awaits me on the other side.

And now, when the countless patients who I see in my profession, moan and cry to be allowed to stay in the world beyond and to not be brought back again, I understand. And I've even changed my medical directive.

Like I said, I don't share this story often. I have repeated it maybe 10 times in five years. Others can say it was sedation, a dream or the mind of a crazy man. But I know the truth, so it doesn't matter. I know how it changed me in my faith and the hope that it has filled me with. I know that at the end of my life, it will be my new beginning.

DINA KUCERA

I need to clarify something ahead of telling this story. I've been high easily a thousand times, possibly five thousand times. When my addiction to opiates became overwhelming, I was buying pills off the street. Even with a prescription that allowed me five per day, every day.

I know the feeling of being high. There is no confusing an opiate high. It's an EXACT feeling every time. For several months before *that horrible day*, I had been buying pills, like I normally did. But for a few months, I was really sick. I couldn't figure it out. It was difficult to walk through the house, or even check the mail.

I was light headed, nauseous and sick. One time I was walking out of the bathroom and thought I was passing out and safely grabbed my bed. There were three occasions where I almost passed out. One of them happened at night, right before I went to bed. I walked toward my husband saying, "Something is wrong," holding the wall. He led me back to bed.

My husband and I were driving to Tempe to have dinner. We passed a restaurant where a friend did a comedy show. We thought about stopping but decided to continue to the restaurant. When we got there we drove around back to park in a dirt parking lot. The moment we got out of the car, there were people everywhere. They were screaming and running over each other with their cars. They were stabbing and shooting each other.

My husband John screamed for me to get in and just as I jumped in the car I was shot in the stomach. I was screaming with the worst pain I had ever felt! We were frantically looking for a hospital.

Then…….something happened that I will remember for the

rest of my life. It was dark - pitch black dark. There was no sound at all. I was leaning back into it and it held me. In this moment I felt breathless because of the encompassing peace. It felt like the safest moment I have ever had. No fear. Only complete bliss, warmth and comfort. It was like wrapping the dark and silence around me like a blanket. I felt perfect. It was indescribable. It was a way of being that I never knew existed.

While I can't feel this way again just by willing it, I will always remember that day.

My daughter, April got to my house and walked into my bedroom. I was blue and not breathing. I must have stopped breathing mid-seizure because my body was contorted in that way. My body was 'frozen'. She couldn't move my arms or my legs. As she screamed she called 911. Then she got the Narcan out of my closet. My head was all the way back and immoveable, my mouth was open as she tried to navigate the Narcan.

The ambulance arrived. It was quite a scene. I didn't have a heartbeat. They asked April if she knew how long I hadn't been breathing. She had no idea, she had found me this way.

The paramedics tried more Narcan. They tried CPR, more Narcan. They got me into the ambulance. More Narcan, more CPR. Nothing was working. My daughter was screaming, telling them, "They had to try again. They had to try harder". Two paramedics had to hold her back.

When we arrived at the hospital, they pumped my stomach and put me on a ventilator. After a few hours I was breathing on my own. When I opened my eyes I tried to scream for help because I had been shot in my stomach. The pain was from my head to my toes. I looked at my arm and it seemed like something was bubbling under my skin. Something really hot; fire hot. My entire body was on fire!

The room was full of people I didn't know. The conversation was confusing. The doctor said it was an overdose but it wasn't a drug I was prescribed. She asked my family if I could have bought something off the street and they all said I could have and probably would have done that.

Finally I began recognizing the people in the room as my husband and daughters. But I was unable to talk. And the pain was another thing I will never forget, it was horrific and mind blowing. Even in that sickness, I thought I wouldn't survive, it would be impossible to live in this much pain.

I said to my daughter, "I was shot in the stomach."

She said, "No mom. You overdosed."

When we went home from the hospital we realized the guy I bought Percocet from had sold me fentanyl instead. Weeks later we discovered he had been selling me fentanyl for months and that is why I was so sick. Every time he sold me the pills he knew they could kill me. The last one I took almost did.

But I still think about that small space of time in the darkness. After a year and a half of not using drugs or alcohol, when I remember that event, I feel as though I was between the gates of Heaven and Hell. Maybe there is a pocket of God's grace, holding me, reminding me that it wasn't God's plan for me that day. That just by way of not loving myself, my insides had become like the violence in that dirt parking lot. Every aspect of my life was desperation and fear.

I believe in God's grace. Grace means getting something you don't necessarily deserve. Because of God's grace I am no longer afraid to die and I am also no longer afraid to live.

It lies about us like a cloud, a world we do not see. But the sweet closing of the eyes may bring us there to be.

Harriet Beecher Stowe

Bits and Pieces

Apparitions - a ghost is the soul or spirit of a dead person or animal that can appear to the living. Descriptions of ghosts vary widely from a visible presence to translucent or barely visible wispy shapes, to realistic, lifelike forms.

According to a 2009 study by the Pew Research Center, 18% of Americans say they have seen ghost.

I really feel this is not an accurate accounting of the number of people who have experienced other worldly encounters with presences seen and unseen.

I have felt certain that I have glimpsed a passing figure, a movement out of the corner of my eye, a flash of someone or something moving from room to room, the feeling of a presence joining me on my bed. Perhaps the spirit of a dog I have lost, or maybe even my son coming to rest his head by his mother. I am firm in the belief that I am not alone in these experiences.

I wrote in my first book, *Trudging Through the Valley of Grief* my grandmother's story of the souls of loved ones passing by a window on her porch. This was how she knew when someone had passed.

Later in this book I will relay my own experiences of apparitions, in Mary's story, that I have witnessed.

Roxanna Carrothers

Chandra Lee Portman

Chandra forwarded the following picture to me explaining it was taken at her parent's home after the death of her mother. There was nothing in the air and no apparent visible reason for the photograph that emerged. Her mother had been a Radio City Rockette, a dancer and her father had been a professional football player. She felt the photo showed them reunited and doing what they loved together.

Mother (left) dancing & Father (right) in football position

Roxanna Carrothers

KIM WHITAKER

It was 1992 on a bright sunny June Alaskan day. I was 32 years old. My boyfriend and I had taken a drive to Portage Glacier along the most beautiful highway in North America. The stretch of curvy and sharp turning highway is between huge beautiful mountains and the ocean.

We had a great time at the park! As we headed north to go home we had the cliffs of the mountain on our right and a drop off with railroad tracks on our left that led to the amazingly beautiful inlet. The two lane highway was busy as usual. In Alaska, we make the most of our time when there is sunshine.

In front of us was a jimmy style truck with the roof off, convertible style. I was thinking how much fun these three young people were having. More than likely they were on their way home after a fishing trip. Fishing gear was visible in their vehicle. Carefree as only the young can be, hair blowing in the wind!

Just before we approached a sharp turn to the right I saw the front left tire of their vehicle fly off the truck, rim and all. It bounced high in the air and rolled down the embankment to the railroad tracks. The truck could not make the turn without the wheel and could only go straight.

The truck could not avoid a four door white sedan coming straight at it. The truck smashed into the sedan's driver side door, then rolled and flipped. The truck then came to rest with it headlights down on the highway, standing straight up with the whole undercarriage facing us. Smoke, dirt and debris flew from both vehicles! The sedan was in the middle of the highway smashed like an accordion. The hood of the car was gone.

When I was younger I was an EMT, so it was common for me to stop at all accidents or medical emergencies, if my skills could be of use. I turned to Mike, my boyfriend, and instructed him, "Find someone who can call 911."

I grabbed some clean cloth out of the glove box and ran for the closest vehicle to me. It was the car. The only part of the car still intact was the passenger's seat. It was occupied by a woman slumped over but she started to move. I opened her door. I only later thought how easy it had been to open, considering the damage. I was assessing her for neck and back injuries so I could get her out when it appeared a fire had started in the engine.

As I turned my head left back to her I was shocked to see a big man crushed in what had been the rear seat of the car. His head was by my left arm. I reached and felt for a pulse. Unfortunately, I didn't find one. Since I had no way to get him out I turned my attention back on the woman in the passenger seat.

I told her that I needed to get her out of the car and that paramedics were on their way. I put my right arm under her legs and my left arm behind her back and lifted her out. I laid her down about 20 feet from the car where she would be safe. After giving medical instructions to a bystander I had to move on to the others from the truck. They had all been thrown from the vehicle and lay on the highway.

When I stood up I looked towards the cliff and saw the man that I had left in the vehicle about 15 feet in the air, slightly tilted forward looking at me. He was like a moving gel. I could see the rocks and cliff behind him. He had a peaceful look on his face. I nodded my head as in saying *I see you.* He nodded back. I felt the presence of a heavenly world between us. The peace on his face was so reassuring.

I needed to get back to the others. Two were serious and one critical.

I relayed to the person on the 911 call that we needed a helicopter. I stayed with the critical patient until the ambulance arrived.

Only one fatality is a miracle considering the damage of the two vehicles colliding at 55 miles per hour.

Another miracle that happened for me that day was the knowledge that *we do have a soul.*

But what had the most impact was witnessing the soul move on after death and the peace that surrounded it.

Roxanna Carrothers

Bits and Pieces

Among the most reported visitations to loved ones are people who receive special messages from parents, siblings and departed spouses.

I remember most vividly a time I was thinking of my mother and was overcome with the aroma of honeysuckle. However, there was no honeysuckle growing in the area where I was. It instantly let me know my mother was near. The only place I associated with honeysuckle was on her front porch, where the honeysuckle grew wild.

Another time, my daughter and I were driving to church, on the Sunday morning of Father's Day. My father had died several years before. A truck roared past in the next lane that caught my attention.

We met again when we were stopped at the same red light. I glanced over, out of curiosity for his need for speed. In the back window of his truck was a huge decal that stated *Member of the Old Bastards Club*. My daughter and I exchanged a knowing look. One of my father's proud possessions was a certificate declaring he was a proud *Member of the Old Bastard's Club*. Dad had his certificate framed and often showed it to guests. It was so nice to realize Dad was letting us know he was with us on that Father's Day.

I have, on several occasions, met people who knew my father. These occurrences wouldn't be strange except I moved to Arizona, over 2,500 miles from his home in Michigan. He lived his whole life in the same small city there. When these things happen, I have the distinct feeling of getting a hug from my father.

We are spiritual beings having human experiences.

SUZANNE MALPOCHER

---

*The most consistent experiences I've had
have to do with electricity; specifically lights and
a request to my departed husband.*

The first experience happened after I was driving home from a bad dental appointment. The second implant had failed and the dentist had to remove the post.

This happened in the winter. The doctor had fit me in his schedule and I had left for this appointment in mid-afternoon. When I finished the appointment, I found myself driving home in the dark.

I remember crying as I drove saying, "Ray, where are you? It's dark and I'm hurting."

When I entered the house every light on the lower level was on!

⸺◦⸱ꙮꙮꙮꙮ⸱◦⸺

Since that time the fake candles in the fireplace will flicker at random. I have had to call the repairman because my upstairs TV would change channels. No explanation. Lights will flick on and off and not just at my house......Ray travels with me as it is wherever I am visiting!

Roxanna Carrothers

BRIEN KEDISH

I have had contact from two people close to me
in quite dramatic ways!

The first experience was about my best friend Erich Vivian. He was well known in our circle of friends because of his wonderful sense of humor. Erich and I were inseparable since we met in 2013. Since meeting we were literally joined at the hip. He was also close with my wife and children. He taught all three of my boys how to play guitar.

We remained steadfast friends until December of 2016. Erich had been sober during our friendship but when he relapsed, it was a struggle for me to even talk to him. He began hiding and isolating, as is common with addiction.

In April of 2018 Erich died in his sleep from and "accidental" overdose.

The night Erich passed away I was asleep in my bed when I was awakened by Erich loudly telling me to "wake up". He always called me by last name.

He kept saying, "Kedish, wake up" over and over. I wasn't sure what was going on or why he was in my bedroom. As I became fully awake I heard his voice again, as if he were in the room, "I just want to thank you for everything you did for me," …..And then there was just silence.

The only person I have shared this with was his daughter but I swear it was as real as any experience I have ever had.

My second story is about my father. My Dad passed away in October of 2017 and shortly after I started having a series of interesting occurrences. I noticed that lights would dim and flicker when I was alone in the room. I'm an architect so I know what it looks like when there is a power surge that causes lights to dim and *this wasn't that*. The lights would wink off and on as if to say "hello". That is how it felt to me. This went on for about a year and it did not matter where I was.

But the most dramatic event that happened was as follows; when I was 11 or 12 my father gave me an ivory handled 13" Italian switch blade knife that his uncle had acquired in World War II. When he gave it to me, he told me the story behind this knife.

My father was born in 1942 so his father and uncles were all in the war. His favorite uncle gave him this knife after the war. It was something my Dad had always cherished, not because he liked knives, but because his favorite uncle gave it to him. So I was honored when he gave it to me.

Eight years later, I was in college and I decided to bring the knife back to school with me to show my fraternity brothers, you know, to look cool and all. Well, not even a week after I was back in school, somebody stole it! I was devastated because it had that generational connection for me.

I never told my Dad that it had gotten stolen but he wasn't the kind of person that would have become upset. He grew up poor and didn't place a lot of value in material things even though he became fairly well off later in his life.

So years and decades go by and I have moved dozens of

times, living in places like Hawaii, Seattle and Phoenix, always wondering what had become of that knife. It never left the back of my mind because it had so much meaning to me. In December of 2017 (32 years after it was stolen in Pullman, Washington) I was out in my garage getting out Christmas decorations. As I was taking things out of bins, I saw something on the bottom of the bin. I reached down and in my hand was the very knife that was stolen 32 years earlier and 1200 miles away.

A picture of my miraculous knife!

This was not a case of something being overlooked on the bottom of that bin for 32 years. The bin was something my wife and I had packed sometime over the past 6 years. Before that my wife and I had moved half a dozen times. Before I met my wife I had moved twice as many times. That knife was stolen, never to be seen again. I never brought it home from college with me.

So, I think my Dad must have somehow placed it in that Christmas bin for me to find!

I have had many people pass away in my life but never did I have contact like I did with Erich and my father.

Roxanna Carrothers

LINDA ELLER

This is a story about my Dad and Him telling me goodbye!

The day my Dad died I was so brokenhearted. I rode with my Dad to the funeral home. I told the driver that I just wanted to know that my Dad was going to be okay. I wanted him to know how much I loved him and that I would always love him.

As I sat in the chair at the funeral home I prayed silently that God would give me a sign that my Dad was going to be okay.

My brothers and I left the funeral home to go to my brother's house to look for a photo of my Dad to use in the newspaper for his obituary. The very first photo my brothers placed on the table for me to see was a photo of my Dad standing in front of a train. He had a smile on his face and he was waving!

I knew immediately in my heart that was my Dad waving goodbye to me. And by his smile I knew he was going to be okay and that he was happy. I knew I didn't have to worry about him.

This is a moment that will stay with me forever! I did love and do love my Dad with all my heart. He called me "LittleLind" my entire life.

God was very good to me for giving me an answer to my prayer.

Roxanna Carrothers

MELINDA RAY MARSH

I thought I had lost my Mother's wedding ring forever.

My husband and I were leaving our Dodgeville home the very next day for our move to Florida. Today was a final inspection before we left.

The floors had been scrubbed and all the final cleaning had been accomplished. On one last final walkthrough I caught a glimpse of something on the tile floor abutting the door jamb.

I bent down and there was my mother's wedding ring! I had lost her ring years before. It was lying on the very floor I had just scrubbed the day before. I never thought I would see her ring again.

I know it will never leave my sight again. I put it on my finger and will never remove it.

I twist it when I am making decisions. I speak to her internally as I ponder the decision.

I feel so loved!

Just one more story of the lost being found! Each story reinforces my own experiences with finding objects I knew were meant for me and found in places where I did not even plan of being. What a great gift to experience these "mementos."

Roxanna Carrothers

SANDRA HARTSBURG

When I was growing up, we got silver dollars for special occasion gifts. My mom passed away in September 2017. I was decorating for Christmas 2017 and moving objects from the bookcase to put Christmas objects on the shelves. On the very top shelf I found a silver dollar! I was floored.

Then when I went into the Christmas box I found two more silver dollars. I just said, "Hi Mom, miss you too!" I felt a great warmth flood through me.

My brother James and I were very close growing up. I was the big sister. He was a Vietnam Vet. He suffered from PTSD. He was very successful but had stuffed these feelings down for years. In the last few years of his life anxiety attacks and the inability to drive made him realize that he had a problem and it motivated him to get help.

After my brother passed, I was vacuuming and had Dr. Phil on television. I stopped to listen to a man who was helping Vets cope with PTSD. I said out loud, "Oh Jimmer, I so wish I would have helped you more. I knew you weren't the same, but did nothing to help you specifically. I'm sorry."

I went back to vacuuming when I heard a loud crash. Some books and other items flew off the shelves of the same bookcase. A picture of my brother and I as young children, landed at my feet.

As that familiar feeling of warmth and love flooded over me, I knew it was a big hello from my brother. I felt that he was letting me know I wasn't to carry that burden.

Roxanna Carrothers

JOANN WALL

I could go on and on since my husband Wayne passed. He has visited me many times. I am aware of his presence when I see the beautiful cardinals on my walks or when I see feathers on my patio.

I've had two dreams of him being right next to me. They seemed more real than dreamlike.

On June 1st, I sent balloons off and headed to the mountains he loved, when a cardinal appeared immediately on my back patio.

Later, I made a trip to the golf course where I would sit and watch Wayne hit balls on the driving range. I sat crying and remembering the happy time we spent there, when I noticed I was being visited by three cardinals!

---

*Many birds including Cardinals symbolize a visit
from loved ones to many of my storytellers. The
importance of the number three is examined
later in Lena's story.*

45

Roxanna Carrothers

LORETTA KOEHNKE

I will probably grieve for my sister Shelly the rest of my life. Some days are harder to make it through without her.

One day last month I was having an especially difficult time. That night when I went to sleep I had a very real dream. My sister came to visit me. She looked so beautiful. She was dressed all in her favorite color blue. She even had on her blue topaz jewelry.

She had come to let me know she was happy and not to worry about her.

When I awoke, it felt like she had truly been here with me. I do believe she did visit me and cherish the wonderful message she gave me.

This is just one on the many experiences I have had throughout my life.

"Every so often your loved ones will open the door from Heaven and visit you in a dream. Just to say "hello" and to remind you they are still with you just in a different way,"

Matt Fraser

Roxanna Carrothers

Bits and Pieces

Psychics - People who possess an ability to see and hear that which is unseen or heard to most people. Perhaps you could say they are those who have a heightened sense of perception.

Although many of the stories exhibit this extraordinary quality, they are distinguished from the true psychic or medium, as their experiences are totally independent of them making the choice to experience their events. However, I can only draw the conclusion that everything that an authentic psychic or medium can do, is possible for anyone, as demonstrated in the stories of these ordinary people.

The true medium is in charge, to some degree, of the experience. They can draw information from people they do not know, in order to benefit the person they are reading.

George Anderson and Teresa Caputo are two well-known psychic mediums, who have been tested and proven to have a unique ability to communicate with the beyond. A quick investigation backs up their abilities.

I will not debate whether these are good or bad gifts. I am sure it has everything to do with how the gift, if indeed it is real, is used. Seers are mentioned frequently in the Bible. Joseph could interpret dreams. The Magi were star readers. The shepherds were told the good news by angels and a star. Simeon foretold of Mary's soul being pierced at the time Jesus was presented as a baby. Many portions of the bestselling book in history mentions many such instances of events before they came to fruition. If we don't believe this gift is alive today, it makes it hard to believe it ever existed, which all faith is based on. *It did and does exist.*

This is also the age of the Indigo children. They are children who are born with extraordinary abilities. One case in point is Akiane Kramarik. She is a young girl born to an atheist mother, who at the age of four, started drawing pictures of Heaven. A search of her fantastic ability makes one certain she has visited heaven.

KAREN HABER

My psychic friend

I grew up the youngest of three children in Massapequa, New York; aka Long Island. I was the only one who would awake in the middle of the night screaming and have to sleep with my parents. I really only started screaming because of the guy I saw sitting on the end of my bed who wouldn't go away when I told him to.

He sat Indian style and wore blue jeans, a red plaid shirt and a cowboy hat. He had brown hair and a moustache. I never found out his name or why he chose my bed to sit on.

I also had dreams that would come to fruition. An example was one where my family and I were driving down a winding dirt road and came to a house. I went inside and into the scary basement where I saw a small blond girl. I had this dream repeatedly for months. One day my Dad took us to a co-workers home that was identical to my dream. I must have looked like Macaulay Culkin in Home Alone going down that driveway. Although upon inspection, the basement was normal, I did encounter a little blonde girl.

My entire family already thought I was nuts so I never revealed to them what had been happening to me. I decided pretty young that I didn't want these things happening to me, so I suppressed and rejected what I now call a gift. Back then I didn't want this gift. Wherever or whomever it came from… they could keep it.

At age 13, drugs and alcohol blocked all of these

experiences. Those things are great blockers of those gifts and great blockers for most gifts from God.

At age 29 I no longer had blockers like drugs and alcohol. Bring on the ghosts! There were many instances, where I knew that my gift was back and functioning. Especially working in a nursing home, I was around a revolving door of death. It had been a very long time since I had actually had one of my experiences with spirits.

My feeling of spirits happens now on a daily basis, thanks to meditation. Meditation is opening a portal for them to come to me.

My most memorable experience is when my mother came to live with me when I was 36. I went to get the mail one day. As I went down the hall and all of the sudden, I smelled the aroma of my great grandparents' apartment in Brooklyn that I had visited in my childhood. The aroma seemed to flood my apartment. I looked to my left, where not so coincidentally was a picture of them hanging between the two bedrooms. My mom appeared to be laying down for a nap, as the door was ajar, and I saw her legs on the bed. I went back towards the kitchen and there standing in the kitchen was mom washing dishes. I am still reeling from the smell because that was new to me, the old familiar smell of an apartment in Brooklyn, some thirty something years ago? And I live on Long Island.

I'm like ..."Uh, weren't you just taking a nap, ma?"

"No," she says. "I was in the bathroom just off the kitchen."

Now I am no longer 6, I am 36, so I laugh it off and say, "Well your grandma is lying on your bed. I guess she came to say *"hello."*

What convinced me this was my great grandmother is when we would visit; she would take us to the back room of the brownstone on Humboldt Street. She would reach up on the shelf and get us the box of toys, where all I would see from a sitting position, were "her legs."

She died when I was 5 years old.

———⚬⚬⚬———

My son was molested at age 5. He informed me at age 7. I was 1 year sober at this time and grateful, as I knew I couldn't have been the mother he needed if I had been drunk.

For the next few years it was a revolving door of doctors, psychiatrists, hospital after hospital, psychiatric centers, an endless list.

After sleepless nights and a lot of crying and praying, one night I actually did get an hour or two of restful sleep. I awoke to a vision of Mary and Jesus at the foot of my bed. I thought I had finally achieved stark raving lunacy for a moment. But then Mary spoke and said, "Everything will be alright." They were both gone before I finished asking, "But what about…?"

Jesus never spoke. I had supposed He was there for support. When I thought about what His mother had been through,

I guess, in retrospect I didn't really have it that bad.

I am in no way a Jesus freak. I don't go to church but I believe He is who He is and that is a fine example to follow.

That was the first time I saw Him, but it was not the last. He has been in my meditation in a glorious white robe with gold trim. The first day I saw Him in my meditation, a friend sent a picture of Jesus wearing the very same thing; a white robe with gold trim.

———∞ᔆᔆ ᔆᔆ∞———

Alcohol and drugs did much damage to my life and relationships. I destroyed my relationship with my father in one phone call, fueled by a case of beer and codeine. We didn't speak for 8 years until I called to tell him I was entering rehab.

But the damage was done. You see my Dad would speak to me on the phone or write me but we never met in person. Over the years I would tell him in my letters, please have someone tell me when the time comes and you're gone from this earth. The time came 9-17-2015. I got a text from my brother-in-law saying his Dad had passed. Then I realized he had forwarded a text from *my* brother. (Another one of my destroyed relationships)

I was at work in an elevator. As soon as I was able, I ran to my car and cried so hard, yet I felt something so indescribably profound. I felt my Dad's presence and a vision flashed before me of a letter he wrote me. Not my favorite letter when I received it, but it is now. He said he was worried about his wife Dorothy when the time came that he passed. If he passed before her, she had nobody to look after her. No kids, no close family. My siblings had nothing to do with her and, yes, this was another relationship I had destroyed drenched in booze.

I heard, "You are the only one who can do this."

I said," Are you nuts? She hates me! We haven't spoken in 30 fecking (Irish) years!" I finally agreed," I don't know how but I'll do it.

"Oh my God, you'd better help me with this."

And so began my story of my journey of healing with Dorothy, per my Dad's request. I had been praying and meditating every day at this point in my life. So, my Dad's gone and he has left me with mission impossible! I am always up for a challenge.

I began by sending her messages via Facebook. I still had a fear that she would hang up if I called, and I was sure she would slam the door in my face if I went to her house. I really truly didn't want to mess this up. This amends was for my Dad.

I prayed every night for Dorothy, I prayed for her to find peace and pictured her and sent her love for almost a month before she contacted me.

It was a bumpy start at first. I told her I was with Dad when he was buried. She thought I was lying because she didn't see me. Dad was buried at Calverton National Cemetery. He was a Navy guy. There they have a service and the burial is hours later. I hadn't wanted to upset her by my presence so I stayed back. I went to find my grandparents grave in the same cemetery.

After I couldn't find their graves, a man saw me and he said that he could tell that I was lost. He gave me the information and then said, "Hey, give me a minute." He also found out where and when my Dad was being buried. He said, "If you wait an hour, you can be with him and even get a viewing." I didn't take him up on that offer, as I preferred to remember Dad as he was.

When Dorothy got angry, thinking I was lying about being at the gravesite, I said to God, you had better take this keyboard and do the next texting or this mission is kaput. Somehow after describing the coffin and knowing the grave number, she knew I was telling the truth. We made plans to go to the grave together as she didn't drive.

On our first meeting, as I ran up the steps to the front door, I felt every resentment and bad feeling melting away with each step. It was an amazing feeling! When she finally opened the door, neither of us hesitated to hug.

Every day after I left Dorothy, I felt my Dad's presence and God's love. Dorothy needed me! We needed each other! She and I healed each other and we talked about it. We had many God winks in the forms of dimes, feathers, butterflies and hummingbirds.

Dad passed one day after his 81st birthday, on 9/17/2015. Shortly after my visit with Dorothy, I received the gifts of dimes and also white feathers (which they say drop from the wings of angels).

I got in my car and there was a white feather on my seat. I got to work and another was on my desk. When I went on a break, another appeared on my dashboard. Then, I found a dime as I was working. This all happened within a few hours - a day or so after his death.

I picked up my stepmother and shared what I had been finding. No sooner had I told her of my gifts, she found a dime. She went to give it to me and I said, "Nope that one is for you from Dad."

She started her own collection of found dimes.

Over the next 10 months I helped teach her to drive and recovered my Dad's Hosta plants. It was a God infused therapy.

Our relationship grew until the day she died in my arms on 7-30-2016.

We were shopping at CVS and she wasn't feeling well. I said, "I'm taking you to the hospital around the corner."

She dropped as soon as we were outside. I caught her from behind. An off-duty fireman walked up.

Her last words were "December 15."

"Her birthday?" the fireman asked.

I felt her spirit leaving her body. I felt the presence of others, warmth and love. I saw the sky get so bright; I knew she was going home.

My first thought was please don't leave me (selfish) then seconds later, Oh God, her journey here is over and boy did it end well!

Flashes of all the healing moments I had with her came flooding in. The time she hugged me and said, "You are my daughter." The many validations of my Dad's love for me, for I thought he didn't love me for almost my entire life. They were priceless gifts.

Days after my mom passed I was at work and sat with two friends for lunch. There were a lot of ladybugs by us and one of my friends said that's a sign that someone you loved who has passed is telling you they are still with you.

As we walked towards the door to go back to work, my friend gasped 'OMG, look at Karen's arm!" They were both covered in ladybugs and not one was on either of my friends.

Bits and Pieces

There is one group of people who are privy to the most wonderful and intimate signs from the other side. Perhaps it is because they stand at the door asking and knocking until they are able to get a message that will carry them to the next moment when they are desperate for more or different answers.

These are the parents who have lost a child or children.

No other group, more than parents, craves the knowledge of where there child is and the knowledge of whether their child is happy or if will they ever see their child again. We bury our elders in a cemetery but we bury our children in our damaged hearts. As with all those who are seekers, they are given so many signs that their child is indeed alive spiritually and will be involved in their lives forever.

We will be introducing new signs and also discussing other familiar signs in the next stories.

One new introduction is orbs...Orbs have so many different connotations and the colors also represent different messages. The orbs denoted in the following stories have meaning to those who view them. Everyone is welcome to their own interpretation but you can't debate the existence of orbs being rather dramatic in the following stories.

We begin so see that God, as a Father, has allowed these intimate messages to be delivered to parents and to those in grief, across the chasm. All of the previous stories are, no doubt, extra gifts to acknowledge that God is God. He is busy turning hearts and minds to His people with compassionate understanding.   To come to the belief that we continue, puts a whole new perspective on what we do and live here.

"This earth is a ship and Heaven is home."

Saint Teresa

LENA CLARBERG KALITOVIC

---

*Since Lena lost her son Troy, the number 3 has
become a source of peace.*

I was grieving so hard this morning and all of a sudden
three hummingbirds came about three feet from my face and
hovered there for approximately a minute. It was such a cool
experience.

There were a few other things that have come in three's.
Today I am three months clean and sober; it has been three years
and three months since I lost Troy. And I continue my journey.

I also have noticed all birds, especially eagles. There is a
bald eagle nest in the tree next to Troy's grave. It was built the day
after his death. There are three eagles in that nest that I see every
time I visit his grave.

---

*Three is the number of perfection or completion.
This number is repeated throughout the Bible as
a symbol of completeness. God's attributes are
three: Omnipotence, Omniscience, and
Omnipresence.*

*And on the third day, the earth rose from the
water, symbolic of resurrection-life.*

Roxanna Carrothers

DONNA MONAHAN

Donnas' story is unique. Her experiences were distinct and intertwined. She lost a child and she also had a NDE (Near Death Experience). She was also blessed by a visit from her daughter in a dream.

My beautiful 18 year old daughter, Tasha, died unexpectedly on August 16, 2009, due to complications from surgery. As any parent will tell you, the grief from losing a child is undefinable. My life changed forever on that day.

The first couple of years after were mostly a blur. I vividly remember two years of praying, pleading, bargaining, imploring and begging God to give me just one more moment with her. Just one more opportunity to touch her, hear her, and inhale her scent.

Of course she didn't come back.

I prayed to God to help me. Help me believe. Help me know she is with me still. *Oh God, this is so hard, I can't do it!*

After Tasha's death some of my health issues became more profound. I started to have heart problems, which led to needing to have two heart valves replaced with mechanical valves. Some of the stitches came out of the mitral valve replacement and I went into severe heart failure. They were unable to repair it so the plan was to convalesce and try to let the body repair itself.

When I was in the hospital recovering from surgery a nurse came in to help me walk. I had a cardiac arrest during our walk. My heart had what is called a complete heart block, which is when the electrical impulses that control the beating of the heart, are disrupted. *I died right then and there.* I completely coded. Because I was in a hospital they were able to start CPR immediately and manual artificial respiration. Within half an hour I was hooked up to machines that took over the beating of my heart and my breathing. I stayed in this comatose state for 5 days before I woke up.

I woke trying to stand up. It was excruciatingly difficult to stand and I remember I had to brush the grass off my pants from sitting in a meadow with my daughter. I looked around and was puzzled. I was at peace but I wasn't standing or sitting in a meadow but lying in a hospital bed. I saw my dear friend Brenda, recognized her and called her name. She jumped up. Shortly the room was filled with people. I couldn't move. I had absolutely no strength and was seeing double.

I was being asked questions. Questions I knew I should know such as who the president was, what year it was, or how old was I? I was unable to come up with the answers. Then they asked if I knew where I was. I looked around and thought I was in just a one-room hospital and I believed it was on an island. When asked again I answered, "It must be Hawaii." That was the only place I could think of that would make sense of the meadows, the scent of flowers and the ocean. When they told me I was in Seattle, I argued, I knew it couldn't be. There were some things I couldn't explain but I knew I was on an island.

I remembered I was sitting cross-legged on a meadow of grass with my daughter sitting cross-legged in front of me. I could hear the ocean and smell the crispness of the air and a fragrant floral scent. I remember two or more other people standing beside us with cloaked faces. The only one I knew for sure was my *daughter* sitting across from me.

I remember her touching my face and saying, "Go back Mama!"

I was happy and at peace but she was encouraging me to go back so I did. I had to stand up to leave her and it was hard, so hard, and *I had to brush the grass off my pants as I came back to this world.*

I wish I had more memories than this but I've made a commitment not to say more than I had actually remembered. It's easy to think I recall more, as I continue to recollect my experience. Many people think it was a dream or it was drugs, but I wasn't on drugs. My body died and I was kept alive by machines only.

The journey back was long and arduous. It was weeks, months and close to a year before I could take care of myself. Tasha's words echoed in my mind through all of my recovery. "Go back Mama." The memory of her voice, her touch and instructions to go back became my mantra and give me strength.

I believe God heard me and He blessed me with ***one more moment***.

About a year ago I had a dream that seemed so real, so genuine; that I doubt it was a dream but instead a visit from my daughter. I was sitting at a large dinner table with many people. I don't know who any of the people were but sitting at the end of the table was my daughter Tasha. Our eyes locked. As I got up toward her, she also got up and walked toward me. We met and our arms encircled each other. As we held each other we started swaying. I felt such love and happiness and I kept saying, "**I got a second chance**."

Roxanna Carrothers

KAREN MALCOLM–SMITH

---

*Karen lost her only child, her son, Dylan, to a
drug overdose on June 5ᵗʰ, 2017.*

I have heard many stories of people who have lost a loved
one and looking back they describe significant events leading up to
that person's death. There had been signs that had been ignored, or
that were not understood.

Roxie Carrothers had given me her manuscript, *Trudging
Through the Valley of Grief,* on the way to the airport for my 21
year old nephew's funeral. I had just recently met her. Roxie was
a true survivor who had found healing in helping others. Frankie,
her youngest child, had died in a car accident 20 years prior at the
age of 21.

Her life was a shining example of hope and recovery. Her
story included a visit to Medjugorje. I knew of *Our Lady of
Guadalupe, Kiehebo, and Fatima,* and the appearances of Mary,
Jesus' mother in other places around the world through history.

But hearing Roxie's personal experience first-hand
brought her story even more to life! So, when Roxie shared how
her silver rosary links had turned to gold and how another woman
and she had witnessed flames illuminating the 16 ton cement cross
on Mt. Krizevac, but not visible to the man standing next to them, I
made my own reservation that same week to go to Medjugorje!

Miracles come in many forms; the signs through nature, electronics, astrophysics, metaphysics and physical healing. But all are conduits to that which begins in the heart. This was my miracle!

I came home from Medjugorje in a state of grace.

A month later, I visited Mayo Hospital for an annual check-up on the pre-cancer Barrett's Esophagus, that I had been diagnosed with the year prior. **The Barrett's was gone!** I was in perfect health. According to the specialist, the very small percentage of Barrett's remissions, are always marked by scar tissue. Mine had none. There was no other explanation than that was a miraculous healing! I collected the medical documentation to add to the numerous healings submitted to the Vatican.

There was something undeniably magnetic about Medjugorje for me. All my life, I had sought and fought the truth within me and somehow, in this little mountain village, the truth found me. There was a presence of overwhelming love all around me. I continued to journey to Medjugorje for the next couple years and found peace, even as I went through a complicated divorce. On the second trip, I had given my child to God.

Seven weeks before Dylan's final day on earth, I took a 12-day sabbatical and had the privilege of attending lectures given by Rochelle Lerner; the renowned Hazelton author on co-dependency associated with addiction. Upon returning home, I called Troy, Dylan's stepfather, from whom I was divorced a year earlier. I asked him to spend the night. I had hoped to share, what I had learned from the lectures with him, because he was also a part of the family's addiction. Although we were divorced, we were very much on a journey of healing together.

Sipping our morning coffee Troy's eyes widened in curiosity as he pointed out some marks on the left side of my face. An obvious imprint from pillows or sheets I thought. But the picture he had taken with his I phone couldn't be explained that simply. A perfect 3D cross to the left and a perfect heart to the right, separated down the middle by what appeared to be a sickle with flames shooting to the top. Remarkable!

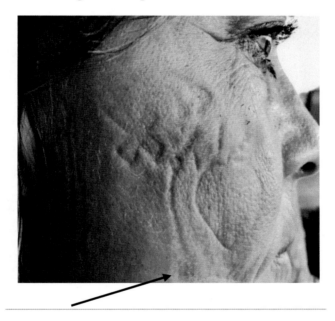

What appeared on Karen's face that morning!
Visible at the bottom center of the photo
(designated by the arrow) of the impression on
Karen's face are these initials IN.

Troy, at that point had to inspect the bed from top to bottom. Nothing! I had to set aside this phenomenon, to jump in the shower and begin my day. But Troy was not able to concentrate on anything else. Troy, being an agnostic, set out to prove an explanation for what he had witnessed. Troy began frantically searching everywhere for an answer, even going through my jewelry, trying to find a match.

It wasn't until my son's passing six weeks later that we realized the "signal grace", (a religious reference to a direct message from God), had appeared on my nephew's birthday. This marked the beginning of Troy's call to faith and a deeper manifestation of my own.

Later, in the Basilica of the Sacred Heart of Jesus in Paris, Troy and I discovered these initials, IN, which had previously gone unnoticed in my photograph. After much googling we discovered IN means Jesus of Nazareth or I am Jesus.

⸺⸻⸺

Always an optimist with a plan, I was certain that Dylan had reached his final bottom in his seven year struggle with opioid addiction. A near fatal ATV accident at 14 gave him his first introduction to mind altering drugs. After a three month prescription of oxycodone and morphine, he was never the same. And neither was my family. Without a medical taper, we can now understand that Dylan was doing the best he could to not be "dope sick." Thus began his marijuana and alcohol usage.

In his first year of college Dylan experimented with opioids at parties with Mathew, his cousin and roommate. Mathew was my sister's only son. After Mathew's death from an overdose, trauma and grief propelled Dylan into addiction. The next step was long term treatment at Betty Ford and sober living. This was interrupted by surgical dental implants and the battle was on again.

During the next three years, he experienced lengthy bouts

of sobriety, along with a return to his participation with family and a love again for his passion for music and boxing. We were infused with hope. And then, relapse again.

Dylan was my precious gift from his father who had passed in a snow mobile accident just prior to Dylan's birth. He always found light in the darkness. Dylan was an extraordinary soul, a man of character, loyalty and honor. I always felt he was "an old soul'. I never, ever gave up hope.

When the call came that Dylan had died from an overdose that afternoon, I knew that suicide was right around the corner.

I found myself acting out my very worst fear; finding my son dead from an overdose. I remembered the voice of God (Rochelle Lerner) from my 12 day sabbatical, interjecting dialogue, about letting go and letting God!

I needed to know that he was with God. Must know! Wait! Was there a God? How could He take the 3 most important men in my life, one by one? Grief heaved from the depth of my soul. What was left of my shattered heart; despair as impermeable as a block of cement. Even in my doubt I grasped my rosary beads, clutched Dylan's Medjugorje crucifix and glued it to my heart.

The weight of shock and sorrow crumbled me into a fetal position for the next few days. Family and friends swarmed the household. One morning, alone, with most everyone on a walk and Troy fighting to get home in a storm from a fishing trip, three blue jays perched themselves on the third story ledge of my home. They were pecking, nearly in unison, on the window pane. My heart leapt momentarily as I "felt" the presence of David, Dylan's deceased father, my nephew Mathew and Dylan. The three loves of my life. I had never seen a blue jay on my property before. And why all three perched together in front of me? Or was I just desperate for a sign?

Following Dylan's service, Troy and I dropped off my brother Roger and his family at the airport, along with our nanny, Mother Gray. She had stayed with me through Dylan's first year following his father's death. Mother Gray was a pillar of faith who called the Holy Spirit down into my living room time and time again. She had been my spiritual council and dear friend through all the years and now had become a pastor. I was frightened they were all leaving. Where to go? Who to turn to?

Troy idled in the departure zone of the airport as we all exchanged final hugs. Returning to the car, my phone, which I had placed on the console, flashed! On the bright screen I saw the definition and uses of "YOU".

YOU – "Are you listening?" "I love you."
YOU – "Together with your close friends and family."
YOU- "After a while, you'll get used to this."
YOU- "You fools!" (As if to say…"If only you knew")
YOU- "The minister was later to be sacked by you-know-who."

Instantly I knew, without reservation, this was from God. From Dylan! "Are you listening?" The seemingly hundred times, he had said this to me, in my previous "important" task filled life. "Mom, are you listening?"

'The minister was later to be sacked'…a strange illustration for a definition. But three months later, the pre-occupied priest, whom we very reluctantly conceded to residing over Dylan's service, was sent away from the parish to another city.

One week after Dylan's passing, Troy, I and a small group of close friends went to our cabin in the woods, a one acre hideaway. With a sense of disorientation from the lingering shock of Dylan's absence, we seemed to wander aimlessly around the bank of the river. Around 11:00 p.m. we were visited by a massive cloud of swallows that took on the energy of a mosquito swarm. They nested a couple of miles down the river where Troy, Dylan and I often passed by boat. The swallows began swooshing between our legs and brushing our faces with their wings. In the wake, of our sorrow, we paid little attention to them, although they were swarming us. The six of us huddled on the bank as Dylan's best friend Jake led us in a scripture that spoke of "fowl." We prayed for a sign and suddenly our friend Eda gasped, "He's here! He is with us!" Without anyone stating the obvious, at that moment we realized we were sitting in the middle of a miraculous phenomenon of nature!

I later learned that as far back as ancient times, **"the swallow was believed to represent God or the soul of someone who died. This spirit bird also symbolizes protection, love and decisiveness. "**

Somewhere along the way, I was developing a stronger consciousness about being present and was experiencing a relief that embraced me for longer periods of time. I found refuge each morning and evening in the guidance of my devotionals and in prayer, which included my own little conversation with God. And there was no doubt He was listening.

Feathers had been turning up in the oddest places; under Dylan's helmet, in his drawer, on my steering wheel, in a book, and a couple times on a chair I sat down on. Usually white. I told my niece, Alexis, about it on her visit to Alaska that summer and I saw the deer in headlight stare that I would expect from anyone. But, by the end of the week and many feathers later, a white feather swirled in front of us and landed smack in the middle of an eye-level spider web as were just passing a building. Alexis looked at me in astonishment and exclaimed, "You really do get feathers!"

One particular morning when the anchor of grief was heavy, I walked down to the 100ft. cottonwood tree on the river's edge to see if its two resident eagles had possibly left something for Dylan's memorial feather bouquet.

With stunning grace, one of them swooned down and dropped a white feather directly behind me on the cabin pavers. Minutes later, Troy came down from the cabin and another landed a second white feather in the same spot as mine! We both laughed the kind of laugh as if we had won the lottery!

Suit up and show up. I had learned this principle in my 12 step program that began twenty-two years prior. It was a stepping stone to a new spiritual design for living, that kept me in hope and healing, as I raised my son as a single parent.

I was now forced to take one day at a time, as I trudged from mass to counseling appointments, grief support and the evening solace I found in reading the Bible. I was desperate to know that God had my son. I needed to know that God recognized that Dylan had a disease that he was powerless over. Why else had 76,000 other people overdosed and died that year in our country? Why else had it been declared a National Crisis?

I decided to go to Medjugorje and ask Mary for an answer. **Demand it.** Otherwise, I would die. Now, with only four months into the loss of my son, my dear childhood friend helped me on the plane, steadying my shaky feet on the one-day journey to Bosnia-Herzegovina. On the way to Saint James church, on my first day there, a picture in a shop window caught my eye. It was a provoking oil print of Jesus holding a completely broken, limp young man from behind. In it, I saw my boy in surrender from his disease. The young man held a mallet in one hand and a nail in the other, indicating that Jesus had died for our sins. I took a picture of the print on my phone and continued on my way to mass.

Six days later, returning from the base of the mountain where the visionaries had received the monthly message from Mary, I trudged back to my room. I collapsed, lying prostrate on my cold floor. Deflated, I cried out to God, insisting that He tell me directly that He had my son! At that very moment, my phone, lying next to me, lit up, opening to the archived photo from a week earlier. It was the picture of Jesus holding the broken young man! I knew that my phone was cleared daily; I hadn't seen the picture since I had taken it. I had taken many pictures since and a light doesn't just come on!

I was certain that God had answered my plea.

Returning to Scottsdale, where I wintered, I joined my weekly Women's AA meeting at which I read aloud a prayer from an encouragement card, someone had given me. "And ye shall rise on eagle's wings."

After the meeting, a young woman named Sandra approached me and asked if I could mail her the prayer I had read. She was newly sober and needing a meeting, found herself in our women's group. This was her first time at this meeting. After the meeting, it was customary to meet for lunch, for those who could go. I invited Sandy to join us and offered to buy her lunch. Grateful, she agreed to join our group. Sitting together, on the end of the table of about twelve women, were Sandy, Leslie, Roxie and myself.

I commented on Sandra's beautiful rosary she was wearing. Thus, the subject of Mary and Medjugorje came up. Sandra's eyes widened when I told her the story and showed her the picture that had appeared on my phone in Medjugorje. I explained, my only concern was that my son had been forgiven.

Wide eyed Sandra reached into her purse and pulled out a pamphlet she had picked up in a bus station. She didn't know why she kept it but she always carried it with her.

Our group of women was all privileged to be a part of the message that came to Karen that day. Her son had indeed been FORGIVEN

Troy and I made a trip to Paris and Jerusalem where my faith was rewarded by continued blessings, that all pointed to fact, that my son by God's grace, traveled with us.

Encompassing four blocks, surrounding the Basilica de Sacre-Coeur was Montmartre, the charming storybook setting of 1920's Paris. It was alive with tiny, crowded cafes, oyster shuckers, barrels of fresh baked breads and art shops, selling the classic prints of Monet, Picasso, Renoir and Van Gogh. With works of the artists, who had once inhabited these very charming cobblestone streets.

A hand carved Pinocchio caught my eye, a childhood favorite of my son's. I made my purchase and bounced along the streets a step lighter! I remembered that I had recorded Dylan's sweet 3 year old voice singing the song from the movie. I replayed the lyrics in my mind.

"I got no strings to hold me down, to make me fret, to make me frown. I got no strings, 'cause now I'm free, I got no strings on me"

The lyrics stopped me in my tracks and nearly ceased my heart! Dylan was not only forgiven, he was free! The binding chains of addiction that ultimately took his life were gone and he was in joy. I shook from head to toe. What more could I, as a mother, possibly ask for? And most electrifying....How great is our God!

On our second night in Israel following Jaffa and Tel Aviv, we joined our travel group, where we experienced sunrise on the

Sea of Galilee, where Jesus walked on water. The spot where Jesus gathered his disciples and led humble fishermen; to become fishers of men. As the sun peered on the horizon, rose hues illuminated the endless sky and grace illuminated my soul. I snapped some photos.

I had promised to share my footsteps with Roxie and texted her and others the beautiful scene from my balcony. A moment later, I received a return text from Roxie. "Karen! What an amazing photo. I see the sun and the Son." And it was true! I had missed it. There in concise clarity was the image of the Son of God standing on the Sea of Galilee!

I continued my tour, breathless.

Now, almost two years later, Dylan was gone and I was making my fifth trip to Medjugorje, following the Holy Land. Always receiving new gifts with each journey to this blessed place, I attended the site where the visionaries were receiving the monthly message of Mary. The message that afternoon was as follows:

Dear Children, My earthly life was simple. I loved life and rejoiced in small things even though pain and suffering pierced my heart. My children, I had the strength of faith and boundless trust in God's love. All those who have the strength of faith are stronger. Faith makes you lie according to what is good and then the light of God's love always comes at the desired moment. That is the strength which sustains in pain and suffering. My children, pray for the strength of faith, trust in the heavenly Father and do not be afraid. Know that not a single creature that belongs to God will be lost forever. Every pain has its end. Then life in freedom begins, where all children come, where everything is returned!

My joy couldn't be contained. I felt the sweetness of being risen up and away from my own personal suffering.

Later that summer, on a particularly sad day of reflection for me, my niece Jesse sent me a picture of her seven month old daughter in a splashing pool. Suspended near the child, a reddish orange orb! Inside the bold framed circle was the perfect shape of a dove against the translucent center. The dove was in the shape of the Holy Spirit.

I reflected on the strong connection that my niece and I share in faith and everlasting life. Her child is our only descendent and Dylan was a strong protector by nature. Through a sense of faith, I felt certain that God was comforting and reassuring me that Dylan remained a part of our family.

———❦❦❦———

It has been two and half years since Dylan left, but my story is not over and neither is Dylan's or any of those who have passed on before me. Our stories are really about love; the finite energy that transcends in, through and beyond time and space and is a channel to those who are open to it. It moves from heart to heart beginning with the love from our Creator. And if anyone pays attention, I believe they will begin to ask Dylan's question......*"How can there not be a God?"*

Just now, as I was coming to the end of this story, my phone dinged. At his time, at this place, a random message from Dylan's dear friend, Marianne; came with an attachment. Now ....perhaps it is Dylan who close this chapter.

WHEN I DIE give what's left of me away
to children and old men that wait to die.

And if you need to, cry,
cry for your brother walking the street beside you.
And when you need me, put your arms around anyone
and give them what you need to give to me.

I want to leave you something,
something better than words or sounds.
Look for me in the people I've known and loved,
and if you cannot give me away,
at least let me live in your eyes and not in your mind.

You can love me best by letting hands touch hands,
and by letting go of children that need to be free.
Love doesn't die, people do.
So, when all that's left of me is love,
give me away.

Meditations Before Kaddish

ROXANNA CARROTHERS

My story has been told in my previous book, *Trudging Through the Valley of Grief.* I am happy to report that the signs and my story did not end when the book was published. In the following three years, the blessings and messages continue to be a part of my life. I now come to expect and cherish each and every message, knowing they all lead me to a more complete understanding of the limited time I am in this world, which is only a drop in the rain barrel of eternity.

The more I understand the Power of the Universe, under the dominion of the rule of the Higher Power, I call God, and I have come to expect nothing less than spectacular! For all the things I have witnessed in my time here, I no longer doubt that anything is beyond His ability: Jonah and the whale, the Red Sea parting, Jesus walking on water, Mary and the Immaculate Conception…Nothing, and I do mean nothing, is beyond belief.

In my chapter on Mary, I will recount some of the things I experienced in Medjugorje. In case you didn't read my experience in my first book, I want to bring everyone up to speed on what the Mother of Jesus is up to in this very special time of grace.

The Book of Stories has made me aware of something I hold dear, that God touching hearts and minds is no rarer than finding a grain of sand on the beach. He is busy sharing love and miracles with His children through every means available to Him, which is limitless. He did, after all, create everything and everyone.

After I read Joe's story and his experience, having had a NDE, his description confirmed a belief that I hold to be true from everything I have learned. His description of being in Heaven was a feeling that he had been in this place before. I hope that one gift of this book is to come to believe, with certainty, that we were created for eternity.

Another such gift to me was on Mother's Day. All of my children were visiting their Father and me in Arizona. It was the first time, in a very long time, that we were all together. They all live in Wisconsin and have children and grandchildren of their own, so the effort to come together was much appreciated. My son Walter was up early on that morning and he was trying to capture the sunrise in a photo. When he shared his picture, I was certain that we had a lot of other visitors on that Mother's Day!

Mother's Day 2019

My second encounter with the "visible unseen" (coining a phrase that covers something that can be seen but yet remains in an unseen realm beyond us), was another very special day for me and mine.

The 4th of July is a very significant day in my life. It is the day my son Frankie, spoke to me for the very last time. (Because he spoke to me the day of the 4th was a gift of grace, to let me know he was okay, although he was killed in an accident early that morning). Frankie came to me while I was praying alone in my bedroom in Wisconsin, after getting the news he had been killed in Florida, early that morning. Kneeling by my bed, I did not look up but felt a hand on my shoulder. I heard Frankie say, "I'm okay Mom. I'm staying for my funeral and then I'm going on!"

This is how I know Brien's Kedish's story experiencing his friend, who had died, waking him up to thank him, rings true to my own experience.

The years, since I lost Frankie, have brought me in touch with so very many parents who have lost a child or children. I have made it a practice to get a photo of the children and placing them on my prayer station, so I can always light a candle and include them in my prayers. Since this book I am including Tasha, Donnas' daughter, among those I pray for. Dylan and Troy are already there along with Zoe, Kolby, friends Donna and Randy and of course, Frankie.

On the 4th of July this year, we wanted to acknowledge Frankie and all of those whose pictures I keep on my prayer station. Balloons were the vehicles we always used to send messages to the Heavens. We have had to reexamine that means for messages, as the safety of animals and other environmental harm has become apparent. So, this year we went with a Chinese lantern.

85

Our *adopted* son-in-law, Glen Schad, did the honors of lighting the lantern and sending it into the sky. I was at the ready with my phone to capture pictures of the lantern ascending into the sky sending the message of "love" to heaven. For some reason I had taken a couple of photos and then my camera jammed. I pressed the button to snap a shot and my camera wouldn't click I hit the button several times and frustrated thought, "Oh crap! I am not going to get any pictures". When we went back inside I checked my phone and realized someone or something else had taken charge of my camera and gave me a special blessing.

Glen

Our Lantern

I think this photo resembles flying doves.

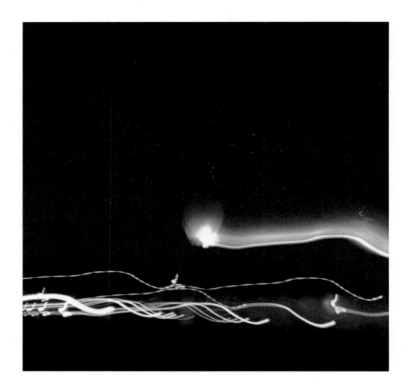

My friend Karen Malcolm-Smith is a pianist. She examined the notes that appear on the lower left of this photo. Her conclusion was that the notes are FC, FC, FC, not realizing what they could mean.

My daughter Michelle exclaimed, "Those are Frankie's initials!" My son's name was Frankie Carrothers!

I could never have created these very special pictures!!

One more dramatic event that could never had happened without an interjection from the "visible unseen". My dear friend Karen Malcolm –Smith is a generous, spirit filled woman. It is second nature to her to think of others ahead of herself. She knew my connection to George Anderson from reading my book and from being my dear friend. She had found out that George was making an appearance in Phoenix to benefit parents who had lost children. This is his calling, bringing hope to parents, that we are family forever.

Karen purchased two tickets to see George in person during this event and she invited me to go, also. Karen had a previous telephone meeting with George. One message she received at that time was that Dylan was holding two M&M's in his palm and said his mom would know what they meant. She did! Dylan wrote, recorded and studied rap and Eminem was his idol and greatest influence. So Karen and I were among the people there who were well aware of George's gift.

After George's gift was explained by his assistant, the audience was instructed to please speak out if George says a name and you have any connection to that name. They further explained George was able to discern if that particular name was meant as a message for you or someone else. I knew from experience that if more than one person recognized a name, George would know who the message was meant for. They emphasized several times to please acknowledge if you relate to a name.

The first name was readily identified as a daughter to a woman in the audience. I so related to this woman and her daughter. George announced this woman's daughter had been "bugging" him for several days, from the other side. She let George know her mother would be in the audience. I recognized this daughter's need to communicate with her mother. I could almost feel her unbridled energy, now that her mother was sitting in the audience.

I had experienced that same energy when the other four families and myself and my daughter Pam, met George, in the home of Raymond Moody, a year after we lost Frankie. The mood on our first evening of meeting George was so overwhelming for George that he had to cut short his introduction to the families, as the "children" on the other side, all wanted to communicate with their parents sitting right before them. The level of energy was so high that a glass covering on a sconce on the wall shattered and fell in pieces all over the floor.

We met George again the next day where George let everyone know he hardly had gotten any sleep as the children were in "high spirits" and were not letting him get much rest. In our private session, my son Frankie expressed he, along with the others, was the cause of George not getting much rest!

So I totally related to this daughters need to communicate with her mother. I gathered the daughter had left under circumstances that she may have made the choice to leave here. She needed her mother to know she was happier than she had ever been here. She was working with animals "over there' and was now at peace and happy. She even intimated that she was able to visit here to match animals with new owners to make sure they were going into a happy home. (I have experienced the feeling that our rescue dog had picked us, but perhaps she was aided by someone we couldn't see, knowing we would give her the healing love she so deserved).

I also could identify with every emotion this mother experienced in receiving this healing message from her daughter. I also knew the daughters urgency of getting her message to her mother now that she had a conduit (George) that could give her a voice. (How can this possibly be evil?)

George called on three more audience members and shared words meant for them. They all confirmed that the messages were meant for them.

George announced that he was wrapping up the free readings. He said out loud the name, "Kevin" that would be his last reading.

Silence.

His assistant announced again, "Kevin."

Silence.

After an uncomfortable moment more of silence, with no one else speaking up, I hesitantly raised my hand.

Of course, I knew Kevin, he was my nephew. He and my son were born within a day of each other. My sister and I were in the hospital together with our sons. Kevin had been killed at eight years old when he was hit by a car while crossing the street. I never knew the extent of the damage that happens when you lose a child until I lost my son. How could I?

I thought, if it wasn't for me, George would know. I acknowledged Kevin.

It was for me!

George let me know that Kevin had messages for his family here. That opened the door for more and more family members and messages to come through. As I confirmed each person, I kept thinking, "but where is Frankie?" And then, the very last person to step forward was Frankie.

He let me know how much he loved me and our family. That he was very happy where he was. The joy of hearing a message from your child cannot be described unless you have experienced it.

Since I lost Frankie in 1993, I have had many years to process grief and move forward with my life.

The first year was spent in seeking a "bigger" God. I believed in God but He was someone that I came to think of as my friend. My God gave me special consideration since I had been busy "about His work" since my sobriety date in 1971. Following a 12 step program I thought, but never out loud, that I had a special dispensation and relationship with God. Life might happen to you but God wouldn't treat me the same as you. I was special. I was special alright! What pride, what arrogance. Do I think God took Frankie to level my pride? Of course not! Frankie died using the "free will" God had given him. Would God deny Frankie the gift of "free will" to make me happy? NO! If He did, He wouldn't be God.

I came to understand, after much searching, that my problem was a God that was so small He couldn't help with a problem the size of losing a child. Someone wisely said, "If you can picture your God, soon He will not work for you".

I began to look outside myself and saw so many people, besides myself, who had lost children. I had kept a daily journal of that long year of searching. After some time I wrote a book about finding my way back to a God that could handle life on life's terms. I shared that message with every parent who lost a child that I met, and there were many. It would eventually become my published book, *Trudging through the Valley of Grief.*

I am remembering at this moment, one message Frankie gave me, at my first meeting with George Anderson. Through George, Frankie stated, "You want to know that I am happy and at peace. That is what I want for you too". How logical that our children want for us the very things that we want for them.

My gift from these experiences has been to allow Frankie the chance to grow where he is, while I have been growing here. If Frankie has to be in Paradise and see his mother never heal from losing him, how can he move on himself? I think if I don't move on and remain in my grief, I stop him from moving on also.

My gift with the reading from George Anderson at our last meeting was the knowledge that my son has grown so much through these years. He is no longer like the first anxious young girl who was the first to come through to her mother. He is so much more mature and at peace. What a grace to see that my son is still on a journey and still maturing and growing! Of course, we do continue!

Of course we will always grieve, but we can allow our children to be at peace. We are secure in the knowledge that we are only separated by a thin wall and very little time. I think when we understand this is a temporary separation, we can continue with our journey here, knowing we will be reunited for eternity. Perhaps another lesson is how necessary that we fulfill our purpose here, so our children are free to "live and grow" where they are now. How sweet the reunion when we meet again!

Roxanna Carrothers

Bits and Pieces

To write about the Virgin Mary is no easy task. To say it is a labor of love makes it, nonetheless, daunting. Mary has come through the centuries as "The Immaculate Conception," "Our Lady of the Rosary," "Mother of God," "Queen of Heaven," "Virgin of the Poor," and as "Our Lady of Guadalupe" to name a few.

A list of countries Mary has appeared in is quite impressive. The list includes the Dominican Republic, Lithuania, United States, Venezuela, Belgium, Mexico, Ireland, France, Portugal, Spain, Sweden, Japan, Germany, Poland and Italy. Many times there has been more than one apparition in a country. She has indeed been trying to get her message to all people, everywhere.

The first Marian apparition in history, Our Lady of Pillar, occurred when she appeared to St. James the Apostle, on the banks of the river Ebro in Saragossa, Spain. Unlike every other recorded apparition, this one took place during the earthly life of the Mother of God, October 12, 40AD. So the woman, who lived in Jerusalem, appeared to James before she died in 41 AD, is the same woman who has been appearing in Medjugorje for the past 28 years and up to the present day. In Medjugorje, Bosnia Herzegovina, Mary is appearing as "Queen of Peace."

This is the Mary I traveled 4,876 miles, to honor and to be with. I knew she was appearing there and I was simply not to be denied being with the woman I loved and who I knew had been there the moment my son left his earthly body. I knew she would be there *because I had asked her to be there!*

After the Russians had left Bosnia, the war continued between the Serbs and Croatians. I went, in June of 1994, while the Serbs and Croatians were having a cease fire, overseen by NATO. The war ended in December of 1995.

I never experienced fear, only the excitement you feel when you are going to visit a loved one. I traveled with a group of Catholics on a pilgrimage. I was the only non-Catholic in the group which never occurred to me, because I had read the messages. She was my Mother, too. Mother to all!

MARY, QUEEN OF PEACE

There is no specific date when the *Dawning of Aquarius* will occur. There are many theories and one is that we are now in that actual age. From the song, based on astrology, we know, *peace will guide the planet and love will steer the stars.*

Judging by this description I can make a case, that Mary, appearing in Medjugorje, is indeed the dawning of the Age of Aquarius. My first clue is; *Peace will guide the planets.* Indeed, Mary proclaimed She is here as *(MIR) the Queen of Peace!* My second clue is; *love will steer the stars.* Revelations 12: "*the great sign of the Woman in the sky clothed with the sun, with the moon under Her feet, and on Her head a crown of twelve stars.*"

Is it any wonder that the signs of heaven are being aligned so everyone who cares to look, wonder and explore, will be able to see them?

Unfortunately, it is also a sad time because we know the Prince of Darkness is doing all in his power to undermine the very time of Grace we are in. Look around. How the times have changed. I no longer recognize the place in which I was born. Life seems to have little or no value. Division is rampant in all areas of the only truly free country in the world. People turn on family and friends because trivial things that separate us seem greater than the real things that bind us. I have lived long enough to have experienced a country joined by love of God, country and freedom…but it seems to be tearing apart at the seams. Neighbors seem to be judging neighbors if beliefs differ! Isn't that what makes a country strong, the diversity? How necessary, in this time of turmoil, we look to light and love, rather than the darkness.

Could there be a more appropriate time for the "Queen of Peace" to appear?

"Love one another, as I have loved you'. The words of Mary's son are falling on deaf ears.

Read, explore, study the words of Mary in Medjugorje, as the scariest words she speaks are," *this is the last time She will be appearing on earth".* The woman who has been visiting earth since 40 AD, has declared, She will not be coming back, once She leaves Medjugorje!

Consider the years She has been here, on this, Her last visit. Oprah had shows on people whose lives were changed by going to Medjugorje. Time magazine has done articles featuring this Holy Place. Numerous other avenues of communication have been devoted to the miracles there, in this day age. How many sources have there been so everyone, everywhere would, in every country and every walk of life would know She is here? As faith is flourishing, conversions are occurring in unprecedented numbers!

I hope this inspires you to study, explore and educate yourselves on the present time we are privy to living in.

Because my journey to Medjugorje is documented in my book, *Trudging Through the Valley of Grief,* I will only cover some of the content here for those who haven't read that book. .

Briefly, my love affair with Mary did not begin as a love affair. My son Frankie had moved from Wisconsin to Florida, the furthest apart we had ever been in his 20 years on earth. Being my youngest of five, he was every bit the baby of the family. We attended the Episcopal Church and both of my sons had been altar boys. So when Frankie left for Florida, a strange thought came to mind. Mary, mother of God had been separated from Her Son, so perhaps, I could pray to Her to keep him safe, while he was so many miles away. How did I equate the death of Her son with the separation I was experiencing, I have no idea? However it came about, I prayed daily for Mary to keep my son safe. So on the early morning of July 4ᵗʰ, 1993 when people at the door woke us from our sleep to tell us Frankie had been killed in a car accident in Florida, I went into all the stages of grief, denial and then came blame.

God was on the top of my list but Mary was not far behind. How could She not protect my son?   And then I remembered she didn't or couldn't protect Her own son! This started a journey to find out everything I possibly could about Her. Much anger, prayer and searching led me to a prayer that is said to Mary. As I was reading *The Memorare,* these words sent a chill through my very being:

> *"Never was it known that anyone who fled to your protection, implored your help, or sought your intercession, was left unaided".*

My soul and heart knew, the moment I read those words that was the reason I had been praying to Her for my son. God knew when his time would be over here, thank God I didn't. He gave me prayers to a woman, Mary, so I would know without any reservation that She had been there in the moment my son left this earth. A Mother was there! His Mother, my Mother! So my love affair with Her began and took me to Medjugorje.

My last mission, in giving you a picture of the Mary I love, is to state emphatically, that you do not need to be Catholic, to experience the woman who stood at the cross of Her son, when He gave Her to the world.

Look at the messages through the years, they are accessible to all, it is so apparent that Mary is Mother to everyone. She states it over and over again. She says, "God does not look at what religion you are. He looks at your heart. Whatever you are, be the best of that". She is here to share God's message of love for all. Most importantly we are loved and God has not left us here unaided.

The miracles I experienced in Medjugorje convinced me that nothing in this world is beyond the touch of God. My last experience I will share for this story is being at the aluminum cross, on the evening of June 25th, 1994 when Ivan, one of the six visionaries, was receiving a message from Mary. You must first know that there is no electricity that runs to Apparition Hill. As Ivan was receiving the message, I saw the cross pulsate a spectacular white glow from the ground to the top. It went out the top and two more times started at the ground and lit to the top. In the dark sky also appeared three burning crosses suspended in mid-air. At the foot of the cross was an apparition, kneeling, and from the outline I knew it was Mary. Ivan gave the message to the crowd and acknowledged that Mary had told him, we would know she was there because of the cross lighting up.

This is the reason for this story....Jesus said, "Stay and tell them what you saw and what I did". I have told it one more time, in the *Book of Stories*.

Bits and Pieces

The decision to end *The Book of Stories*, with Elizabeth Kubler-Ross, came early, while this book was just a thought. Towards the end of the book I began to rethink the choice of ending the book with her story. After an extensive search of her work and learning she lived, died and was buried in Scottsdale, AZ, it became clear that *she* had chosen to be added to the stories in my book. I live here and write here and have no doubt she is my angel of inspiration for the topic herein.

She is one, among many intellectual giants, who explored life after life.

"I can never lose one whom I have loved unto the end; One to whom my soul cleaves so firmly that it can never be separated, does not go away, but, only goes before."

St. Berard of Clairvaux

"I have found a desire within myself that no experience in this world can satisfy; the most probable explanation is that I was made for another world."

-C.S. Lewis

—❦❦❦—

"Those who can hear will hear. Those who can't will be pleasantly surprised when they make their own transition."

Elizabeth Kubler- Ross

—❦❦❦—

"Death is nature's way of saying, 'Your table is ready.'"

Robin Williams

ELIZABETH KUBLER-ROSS

Before I share the many beautiful quotes of Elizabeth Kubler-Ross, I will begin with a story as she related it:

While traveling around the country lecturing, I grew tired of repeating the same speech over and over. I quietly said to myself, "Oh God, why don't you send me somebody who has had a NDE (near death experience) and is willing to share it with the audience so I can take a break?"

At that very moment an organizer from the group gave me a little slip of paper with an urgent message on it. It was from a man from the bowery who begged to share his NDE with me. I sent a messenger to his hotel. After a speedy cab ride, the man appeared in the audience. Instead of being a bum as he described himself, he was a rather well dressed, sophisticated man. When he went on the stage, I encouraged him to tell the audience about his experience.

His experience follows as told by Elizabeth Kubler-Ross;

"He told how he been looking forward to the weekend family reunion, how his entire family had piled into a family van and were on the way to pick him up when this tragic accident occurred which burned his entire family to death. He shared the shock and numbness, the utter disbelief of suddenly being a single man, of having children and suddenly becoming childless, of living without a single close relative. He told of his inability to come to grips with it. He shared how he changed from a money-earning, decent, middle-class husband and father to a total bum, drunk every day from morning to night, using every type of drug and trying to commit suicide and yet never able to succeed. His last recollection was that after two years of literally bumming around, he was lying on a dirt road, at the edge of a forest, drunk and

stoned, as he called it. Trying desperately to be reunited with his family and not wanting to live, he didn't even have the energy to move out of the road, when he saw a big truck coming towards him and running over him.

It was at that moment that he watched himself in the street, critically injured, while he observed the whole scene of the accident from a few feet above. It was then his family appeared in front of him, in a glow of light with an incredible sense of love. They had happy smiles on their faces, and simply made him aware of their presence, not communicating in any verbal way, but in the form of thought transference, sharing with him the joy and happiness of their present existence. "

This man was not able to tell us how long this reunion lasted. He was so awed by his family's health, their beauty, their radiance and their total acceptance, peace, and unconditional love. He made a vow not to touch them, not to join them, but to re-enter his physical body so that he could share with the world what he had experienced. It would be a form of redemption for his two years of trying to throw his physical life away. It was after this vow that he watched the truck driver carry his totally injured body in to the car. He saw an ambulance speeding to the scene of the accident, he was taken into the hospital's emergency room and he finally re-entered his physical body, tore off the straps that were tied around him and walked out of the hospital. He never had delirium tremens or any aftereffects from the heavy abuse of drugs and alcohol. He felt healed and whole, and made a commitment that he would not die until he had the opportunity of sharing the existence of life after death with as many people as would be willing to listen.

By allowing him to share with my audience he was able to keep the promise he made at the time of his short, temporary, yet happy reunion with his entire family.

To my readers, because I read his story and shared it, I hope I have allowed him to continue to honor his commitment!

The following are a few of Elizabeth Kubler-Ross' observations of life after spending her life studying death, dying and NDE's:

We need to teach the next generation of children from day one that they are responsible for their lives. Mankind's greatest gift, also its greatest curse, is that we have free choice. We can make our choices built from love or from fear.

It is only when we truly know and understand that we have a limited time on Earth—and that we have no way of knowing when our time is up, that we will begin to live each day to the fullest, as if it was the only one we had.

The ultimate lesson all of us have to learn is unconditional love, which includes not only others, but ourselves as well.

There is no need to go to India or anywhere else to find peace. You will find that deep place of silence right in your room, garden or even your own bathtub.

It is not the end of the physical body that should worry us. Rather, our concern must be to live while we're alive- to release our inner selves from the spiritual death that comes with living behind a façade designed to conform to external definitions of who and what we are.

I've told my children that when I die, to release balloons in the sky to celebrate that I graduated. For me, death is a graduation.

We run after values that, at death, become zero. At the end of your life, nobody asks you how many degrees you have, or how many mansions you built, or how many Rolls Royce's you could afford. That is what dying patients teach you.

There is no joy without hardship. If not for death, would we appreciate life? If not for hate, would we know the ultimate goal is love?

People are like stained-glass windows. They sparkle and shine when the sun is out, but when the darkness sets in their true beauty is revealed, *only if there is light from within.*

You are not a powerless speck of dust drifting around in the wind...we are, each of us, like beautiful snowflakes-unique, and born for a specific reason and purpose.

Mourning can go on for years and years. It doesn't end after a year, that's a false fantasy. It usually ends when people realized that they can live again, that they can concentrate their energies on their lives as a whole, and not on hurt and guilt and pain.

Whether you know it or not, one of the most important relationships in your life is with your Soul. Will you be kind and loving to your Soul, or will you be harsh and difficult? Many of us unknowingly damage our Souls with our negative attitudes and actions or by simple neglect. By making the relationship with your Soul and important part of your life, however, by honoring it in your daily routine, you give your life, you give your life greater meant and substance. Use your experiences, all of them, as opportunities to nourish your Soul!

And after your death, when most of you for the first time realize what life here is all about, you will begin to see that your life here is almost nothing but the sum total of every choice you have made during every moment of your life. Your thoughts, which you are responsible for, are as real as your deeds. You will begin to realize that every word and every deed affects your life and has also touched thousands of lives.

A story told by Elizabeth Kubler-Ross in 1988

You remember when I insisted
we go to the beach
and you said: "No, it's gonna rain."
and I absolutely insisted
and you said: "it's gonna be a horrible day"
and you didn't want to go. But I insisted
and we went and it was a horrible day
and it rained all day.
I thought you were really gonna give me hell for it.
But you didn't
Remember when I tried to make you jealous
and I went out with another boy?
I thought: This time you are really gonna
drop me.
But you didn't
Remember when I demanded that we go
to this dance, and you didn't want to go
but I demanded it? I also forgot to tell you
that it was formal and you came in jeans!
I thought you were gonna kill me.
But you didn't.
I wanted to tell you all these things
when you came home from Vietnam.
But you didn't!

Roxanna Carrothers

ACKNOWLEDGEMENTS

To all my storytellers, you have enriched my journey here by sharing your stories with me. I am honored to be entrusted with your most treasured memories and hope I have treated them with the respect and love they deserve.

—∞❦❦❦❦∞—

To my children: *You are the wind beneath my wings.*

—∞❦❦❦❦∞—

Pam, your support and last minute editing is so appreciated. I respect you as a woman of integrity, love and intelligence. You were my first child and I have been blessed to be your mother.

—∞❦❦❦❦∞—

Bobbi, you always encourage and love me without reservations. That is a rare gift to have from anyone, especially a child. I look to you as my spiritual and moral teacher. You are light years ahead of me in those areas.

—∞❦❦❦❦∞—

Michelle, you are my biggest fan and hugest promoter. You work so hard to support, encourage and share all that I do. Your enthusiasm, untiring work on my behalf is truly a gift any parent would cherish and I do.

—∞❦❦❦❦∞—

Walter, how did I ever win the lottery as a parent to draw you as my son? You have the kindest, purest heart and I am so fortunate that you're in my life. You do your utmost for your family and it extends to everyone you know. So many people are touched by your kind heart and caring.

—∞☙☙❧❧∞—

Frankie, you are my teacher, my guide and all I do is because you are in my life. Even though I cannot see you, I receive all the love and messages you send me. You continue to introduce me to countless people, as you grow on the other side, I grow here with your assistance. *Only a rose.*

—∞☙☙❧❧∞—

To my husband, Bob, who has pulled extra duty cleaning and cooking thus allowing me the time to devote to this project and most importantly because you believe in me, thank you!

—∞☙☙❧❧∞—

To my friend Karen Malcolm-Smith, this is also your book of stories. Your time and effort and editing has been so appreciated. Our stories, hearts and journey are intertwined with one another.

—∞☙☙❧❧∞—

ABOUT THE AUTHOR

Roxanna Bennett Carrothers lives with her husband Robert in Scottsdale, AZ. They moved to Wisconsin and raised their five children there. After selling their Drywall and Painting Company they moved to Arizona to retire in 2007.

Since being in Arizona, Roxanna has been involved in Greater Phoenix writing groups and she has published poetry in various local writer's magazines.

Roxanna has been an active member of a 12 step program for 48 years.

Her other books include: *Trudging Through the Valley of Grief* and *God's Panacea.*

The Book of Stories is Roxanna's latest offering and has been a labor of love for her.

Made in the USA
Coppell, TX
10 January 2020

14349352R00074